MY FIRST BOOK OF
DINOSAURS

WRITTEN BY ANNABEL GRIFFIN
ILLUSTRATED BY ANDREA CASTRO NARANJO

CONTENTS

Words in BOLD can be found in the glossary.

WHAT ARE DINOSAURS?

Dinosaurs were AWESOME!

There were lots of different types, from mighty meat-eating hunters, with sharp claws and teeth, to peaceful plant-eaters.

Long, long ago

They ruled the world millions of years ago, long before humans came on the scene.

Record breakers

The largest animals to ever walk on Earth were giant plant-eating dinosaurs. They stretched above the treetops and could weigh more than 14 elephants! Dinosaurs weren't all big though. Some were no bigger than a pigeon.

Did you know?

The word "dinosaur" means "terrible lizard".

TYRANNOSAURUS REX
tie-RAN-oh-SORE-us rex

A FEROCIOUS hunter!

Tyrannosaurus rex, or T.rex for short, is one of
the best known, and most feared, dinosaurs!
This big, scary dinosaur hunted other dinosaurs,
such as Triceratops.

Big, sharp teeth

Arms too short to
reach its mouth

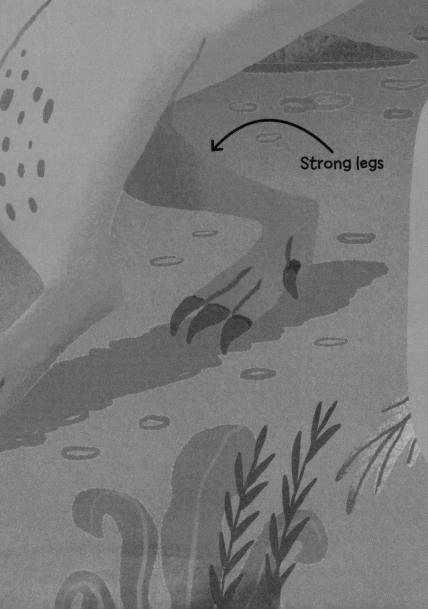

Powerful tail

Strong legs

DID YOU KNOW?

I ate... meat. I was a **carnivore**.

I lived... 68-66 million years ago (late Cretaceous period).

I was found in... the USA and Canada.

This is how big I was:

STEGOSAURUS

STEG-oh-SORE-us

SLOW and STEADY!

Stegosaurus was a large dinosaur that lived in family groups.
Scientists still aren't sure what the plates on its back were for.
They might have been used for protection against **predators**.

Tail spikes
for protection

DID YOU KNOW?

I ate... plants. I was a **herbivore**.

I lived... 155–145 million years ago
(late Jurassic period).

I was found in... the USA and Portugal.

This is how big I was:

Large, bony plates
along its back

Tiny brain, the
size of a lime

TRICERATOPS

tri-SER-a-tops

Famous for its LARGE HORNS!

Triceratops was a similar size to an African elephant. Scientists think that its fancy neck frills were used to show off in front of other Triceratops. It lived at the same time as the T.rex.

Scaly skin

Bird-like beak

Neck frill

Long horns

DID YOU KNOW?

I ate... plants. I was a herbivore.

I lived... 68-66 million years ago
(late Cretaceous period).

I was found in... the USA.

This is how big I was:

SPINOSAURUS
SPINE-oh-SORE-us

Known for its POWERFUL jaws!

This snappy dinosaur might have been the longest ever meat-eating dinosaur. It probably lived near water and mostly ate fish. No one knows why it had the large "sail" on its back, but it might have been to attract other Spinosaurus, or to control its body heat.

Long, narrow head

Long, snappy jaws, like a crocodile

Large "sail" along its spine

DID YOU KNOW?

I ate... mostly fish. I was a **piscivore**.

I lived... 100-93 million years ago (late Cretaceous period).

I was found in... North Africa.

This is how big I was:

VELOCIRAPTOR

vel-OSS-i-rap-tor

A Speedy and athletic HUNTER!

Velociraptor was about the size of a wolf, but its bite
was as strong as a lion's! It had a lot in common with
modern day birds but couldn't fly.

DID YOU KNOW?

I ate... meat. I was a carnivore.

I lived... 74-70 million years ago
(late Cretaceous period).

I was found in... Mongolia and China.

This is how big I was:

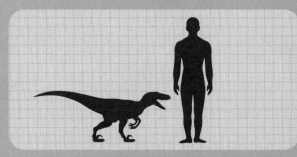

Covered in feathers

Razor-sharp teeth

Large attack claw
on each foot

19

DIPLODOCUS

dih-PLOD-uh-kus

This dinosaur was LONGER than a tennis court!

Diplodocus used its long neck to reach leaves from very tall trees, like giraffes do today. Its teeth were very weak and fell out once a month, so Diplodocus needed to keep growing new ones!

Long neck

Spikes along neck, back, and tail

Long, whip-like tail that could fight off attackers

DID YOU KNOW?

I ate... plants. I was a herbivore.

I lived... 155-145 million years ago (late Jurassic period).

I was found in... the USA.

This is how big I was:

ANKYLOSAURUS

AN-kee-low-SORE-us

Bony plates for PROTECTION!

There was no messing with this dinosaur! It was covered in bony spikes and plates to protect its body from attack. Ankylosaurus could swing its heavy tail to defend itself from predators. It would have packed quite a punch!

Bony spikes and plates

Pointy beak

Heavy club made of solid bone

DID YOU KNOW?

I ate... plants. I was a herbivore.

I lived... 74–67 million years ago (late Cretaceous period).

I was found in... the USA and Canada.

This is how big I was:

PARASAUROLOPHUS
PA-ra-saw-ROL-off-us

This dinosaur is UNMISTAKABLE!

It had a large and unusual head crest. The crest was hollow, with tubes connecting to its nostrils. It probably acted like a trumpet, giving Parasaurolophus a loud call that it could use to send messages to other members of its **herd**.

Could walk on two or four legs

Duck-like beak

DID YOU KNOW?

I ate... plants. I was a herbivore.

I lived... 76-74 million years ago (late Cretaceous period).

I was found in... the USA and Canada.

This is how big I was:

Large head crest was part of its skull

ARCHAEOPTERYX

AR-kee-op-TE-rix

BIRD or dinosaur?

Archaeopteryx was a small bird-like dinosaur that lived at the same time as Allosaurus. Scientists believe that Achaeopteryx was able to fly, but probably not very far.

Bird-like, feathered wings

Long claws on its wings

Unlike modern birds, it had teeth!

DID YOU KNOW?

I ate... meat. I was a carnivore.

I lived... 147 million years ago
(late Jurassic period).

I was found in... Germany.

This is how big I was:

IGUANODON

ig-WHA-noh-don

A fascinating FIND!

Iguanodon was one of the first dinosaurs ever discovered! It got its name because it had teeth similar to an iguana. It spent most of its time on all fours but could probably run on just its back legs, too.

Hard beak

Spikes on the end of its thumbs for fighting off predators

Stiff tail

DID YOU KNOW?

I ate... plants. I was a herbivore.

I lived... 140-110 million years ago
(early Cretaceous period).

I was found in... Belgium and the UK.

This is how big I was:

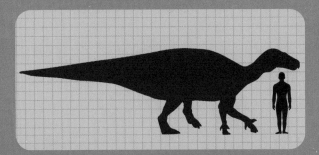

PACHYCEPHALOSAURUS

pack-ee-SEF-al-oh-SORE-us

A TOUGH skull!

This dinosaur is famous for its extra thick, domed skull.
From the size of its head, you might think this dinosaur
had a large brain, but it was actually tiny! No one
knows for sure what its thick skull was for, but one
idea is that they butted heads with each other.

Small horns and
bony spikes around
the head and beak

Walked on
two legs

DID YOU KNOW?

I ate... plants. I was a herbivore.

I lived... 76-65 million years ago
(late Cretaceous period).

I was found in... the USA and Canada.

This is how big I was:

Thick skull, like
a helmet

PTERANODON

teh-RAN-oh-don

Flying FISH-EATERS!

Pteranodons weren't actually dinosaurs. They were a type of **pterosaur**, which were flying **reptiles** that were closely related to dinosaurs. They lived near the sea and mostly ate fish. They flew over the sea in search of fish to scoop up in their large beaks. It is thought that they flew in huge **flocks**.

Furry body

Large wings

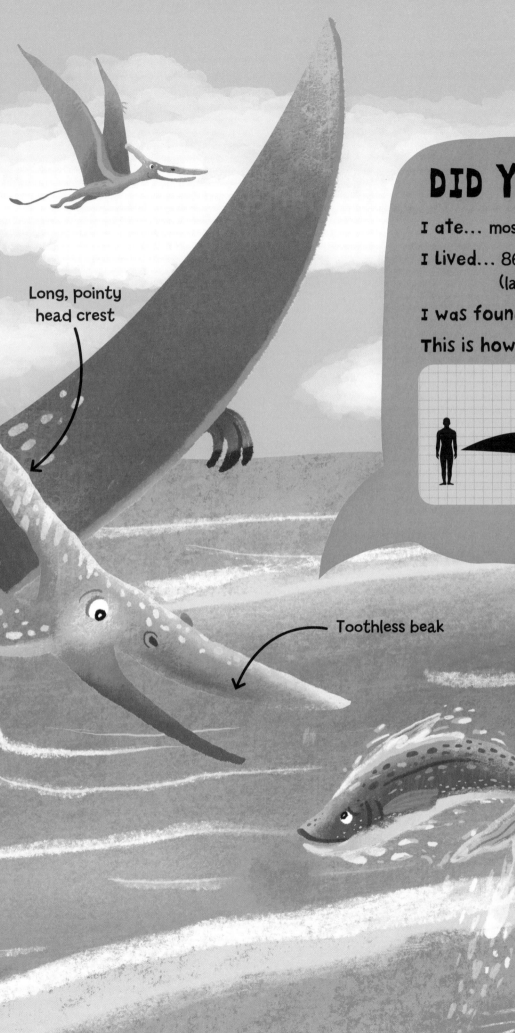

Long, pointy head crest

DID YOU KNOW?

I ate... mostly fish. I was a piscivore.

I lived... 86-84 million years ago (late Cretaceous period).

I was found in... the USA.

This is how big I was:

Toothless beak

PLESIOSAURUS

PLE-see-oh-SORE-us

A real-life SEA MONSTER!

While dinosaurs roamed the Earth, Plesiosaurus was swimming in the ocean. It was a long-necked reptile that would have eaten sea creatures, like clams, snails, and fish.

Wide body, like a turtle

Paddle-shaped flippers to help it move through the water

DID YOU KNOW?

I ate... mostly fish. I was a piscivore.

I lived... 199-175 million years ago (early to mid Jurassic period).

I was found... worldwide.

This is how big I was:

Long, flexible neck

Small head

ARGENTINOSAURUS

AR-gen-TEE-no-SORE-us

A gentle GIANT!

Argentinosaurus may have been the largest animal
to have ever walked the Earth! Only a few bones have
been discovered, so scientists can't be sure of its exact
size. Scientists think it was incredibly heavy, and could
have weighed as much as 14 African elephants!

A slow-moving dinosaur

Big,
stumpy legs

Super long neck for reaching tall branches

DID YOU KNOW?

I ate... plants. I was a herbivore.

I lived... 90 million years ago
(late Cretaceous period).

I was found in... Argentina.

This is how big I was:

ALLOSAURUS

AL-oh-SORE-us

A POWERFUL PREDATOR!

Allosaurus roamed the Earth 76 million years before
T.rex came on the scene. It hunted other dinosaurs, like
Stegosaurus. It was a fast **sprinter** and could open its
jaws really wide to slash at its prey with its teeth.

Bony brows

Sharp teeth

Powerful claws for catching prey

DID YOU KNOW?

I ate... meat. I was a carnivore.

I lived... 156-144 million years ago (late Jurassic period).

I was found in... Portugal and the USA.

This is how big I was:

WHEN DID DINOSAURS LIVE?

Dinosaurs lived a very, VERY long time ago! The first dinosaurs appeared on Earth around 245 million years ago. They roamed the planet for a very long time, until about 66 million years ago, but not all types of dinosaurs were around at the same time.

Triassic Period
(252-201 million years ago)

The very first dinosaurs appeared during this period. Most of them aren't as famous as dinosaurs that came later.

Archaeopteryx

Plateosaurus

Allosaurus

Herrerasaurus

Lystrosaurus

Plesiosaurus

Jurassic Period (201-145 million years ago)

Lots of different dinosaurs arrived during this period, including Allosaurus and Diplodocus.

Cretaceous Period (145-66 million years ago)

T.rex, Spinosaurus, Triceratops, and many other famous dinosaurs were around during this period.

Pteranodon

Diplodocus

Spinosaurus

Triceratops

Stegosaurus

Velociraptor

Tyrannosaurus rex

NOT TO SCALE

LIFE AFTER DINOSAURS

How do we know about dinosaurs?

The only reason we know about dinosaurs is because of fossils that have been discovered. Scientists can learn a lot from fossils, but there is still so much we don't know about dinosaurs.

What's a fossil?

Fossils are remains of dinosaurs like bones and teeth, or marks that they made like footprints. Fossils have been buried and **preserved** under layers of earth and rock for millions of years.

What happened to the dinosaurs?

Most scientists believe that Earth was hit by a giant **meteorite** 66 million years ago. The damage it caused killed off most of the big animals at the time, including dinosaurs.

Do dinosaurs still exist?

You won't see a giant T.rex walking on Earth today – thank goodness! But that doesn't mean all dinosaurs have completely disappeared. Believe it or not, modern birds are really living dinosaurs!

INDEX

First published in 2024 by Hungry Tomato Ltd.
F15, Old Bakery Studios, Blewetts Wharf,
Malpas Road, Truro, Cornwall, TR1 1QH, UK.

Thanks to our creative team:
Editor: Holly Thornton
Senior Designer: Amy Harvey

Copyright © 2024 Hungry Tomato Ltd

Beetle Books in an imprint of Hungry Tomato.

A CIP catalog record for this book is available from the British Library.

ISBN:
9781915461155

Printed and bound in China

Discover more at
www.hungrytomato.com
www.mybeetlebooks.com

GLOSSARY

Carnivore - an animal that mostly eats meat.

Flock - a group of animals that hunt and live together.

Herbivore - an animal that only eats plants.

Herd - a group of animals of one kind that live or travel together.

Meteorite - a chunk of rock that has fallen to Earth from space.

Piscivore - a type of carnivore (see above) that mostly eats fish.

Predators - animals that hunt and kill other animals for food.

Preserved - something that has been protected from harm, decay, or destruction.

Pterosaur - a group of flying reptiles (see below), closely related to dinosaurs.

Reptile - a group of cold-blooded animals, including snakes, lizards, crocodiles, and dinosaurs.

Sprinters - people or animals who can run very fast for short distances.